# Hickory D...

Written by Hilary Minns
Illustrated by Jan Lewis

Collins *Educational*
An imprint of HarperCollins*Publishers*

Little Bo-Peep has lost her sheep,
And doesn't know where to find them.
Leave them alone,
And they'll come home,
Bringing their tails behind them.

Jack and Jill,
Went up the hill,
To fetch a pail of water.

Jack fell down,
And broke his crown,
And Jill came tumbling after.

Hickory, dickory, dock,
The mouse ran up the clock.

The clock struck one.
The mouse ran down,
Hickory, dickory, dock.

Mary had a little lamb,
Its fleece was white as snow,
And everywhere that Mary went,
The lamb was sure to go.

Tim

Mary

Humpty Dumpty sat on a wall,
Humpty Dumpty had a great fall.
All the King's horses
And all the King's men
Couldn't put Humpty together again.

Hey, diddle, diddle,
The cat and the fiddle,
The cow jumped over the moon.
The little dog laughed
To see such sport,
And the dish ran away with the spoon.

Little Jack Horner
Sat in the corner,
Eating his Christmas pie.
He put in his thumb,
And pulled out a plum,
And said, "What a good boy am I!"